Salmon Story

Salmon

BRENDA Z. GUIBERSON

With illustrations by the author

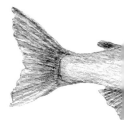

Story

A REDFEATHER BOOK
Henry Holt and Company
New York

Henry Holt and Company, Inc. *Publishers since 1866*
115 West 18th Street/New York, New York 10011

Henry Holt is a registered
trademark of Henry Holt and Company, Inc.

Library of Congress Cataloging-in-Publication Data
Guiberson, Brenda Z.
    Salmon story / by Brenda Guiberson; with illustrations
by the author.
        p.   cm. — (Redfeather books)
    Includes index.
    Summary: Describes the salmon's life journey to the sea
and back, and the threat posed by pollution, commercial fishing,
and other factors.
    1. Pacific salmon—Juvenile literature.   2. Pacific salmon—
Northwest, Pacific—Juvenile literature.   3. Pacific salmon—
Effect of habitat modification on—Juvenile literature.
4. Pacific salmon—Life cycles—Juvenile literature.
5. Fishery conservation—Northwest, Pacific—Juvenile literature.
[1. Salmon.   2. Ecology.]   I. Title.   II. Series.
QL638.S2G94   1993   597'.55—dc20   93-1360

ISBN 0-8050-2754-8
First Edition—1993
Printed in the United States of America
on acid-free paper.∞
10   9   8   7   6   5   4   3   2   1

*For all the people,
everywhere, hard at work
on the salmon rescue plan*

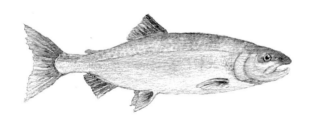

Contents

Salmon Cycle

The Pacific salmon is an amazing fish, able to leap high into the air, change color and shape, and wiggle across shallow rocks if the water is not deep enough to swim. And that's not all. The salmon can travel thousands of miles in both salt and fresh water and then find its way back to the exact stream where it was born. There, with a hard swish of a tail, the female even knows how to dig a nest out of gravel.

For thousands of years, the salmon managed to do all these things without too many problems. Sometimes a flood or drought could make life extra difficult. But then, over a hundred years ago, the salmon started to disappear. Some runs of the fish have become extinct, others are almost extinct, and many are in serious danger.

Now the salmon is the center of a huge rescue plan, the middle of hot discussions about what can be done and how to do it. What has happened to the salmon, the fish that is so important to the people of the Pacific Northwest? To understand the problems for the salmon, it is first necessary to know its cycle of life, each little part, from the beginning to the very end.

The salmon cycle usually begins in the winter in the cool, fresh water of a mountain stream. Round, pink salmon eggs are buried in the gravel at the bottom. Every fish in the stream would like to eat these eggs if they could just find them. Fortunately the eggs are well hidden in a nest built by a female salmon several weeks before.

Some of the eggs are beginning to hatch. Out come tiny fish called alevin. They are pink and very fragile and have yolk sacs attached to their stomachs. This is their food, a perfect food for baby salmon. The alevin stay hidden in the gravel for several more weeks, breathing oxygen from the clear water that flows around them. Every day they grow a little bigger as they use up the food in the yolk sac.

Something else is happening with these alevin. They notice the special chemical smell of the rocks and plants and water around them. It is a smell that belongs only to this stream. No other stream has the exact same things in it or can smell quite the same. The baby salmon have a place in their brain that does nothing but remember

Alevin with yolk sac. *Copyright Mark V. Batur.*

this smell. It is something they will never forget.

By springtime the fish, now called fry, are big enough to come out of hiding. The yolk sacs are all used up. The salmon are about one inch long and as thin as a pine needle. They are silver and are beginning to grow scales to protect their bodies. There is also a slimy layer of mucus over the scales. This mucus helps the fish slide through the water and protects them from disease.

These fish eat tiny plankton that flow by in the current. They must be quick and careful because every big fish, like trout and char, would like to eat them. So would birds like herons and ducks, gulls and kingfishers. The tiny fry look for pools and hidden places around tree roots where they can rest and stay out of the main current. Not many of them survive.

Other kinds of salmon fry might stay in a stream for many months, but these tiny fish stay only a few days. When they feel a rush of water from melting snow and heavy rain, they begin to make another big change. They

Sockeye smolt. *Copyright Gregory T. Ruggerone.*

flow with the current away from the stream, out into a river, on a journey that will take them all the way to the ocean.

As they travel the fry become smolt, a new stage in the salmon cycle. Their bodies lose the little stripes that helped them blend in with gravel. Now they become blue-green on top, silvery-white on the bottom to make them harder to see in the ocean. Soon they will be drinking salty water, and their skin and kidneys must make big changes to get rid of the extra salt. The trip to the ocean must be done in a few days or the salmon will lose the urge to change. This time the journey is fast. A surging flow of water carries them quickly downriver to the ocean. Some survive, and some are eaten by hungry fish and birds along the way.

By the time the smolt reach the ocean, most of them are ready to live in salt water. Sometimes they spend extra time at the mouth of the river getting used to the change from fresh water to salt. They find many new things to eat, like tiny shrimps and crabs. Some fish die because their bodies cannot make this change. It is an-other part of the danger and difficulty of the salmon cycle.

Gradually the salmon swim far out into the ocean and grow much bigger with all the new things to eat. Some stay for a year or two, others much longer. Soon they are eating herring, candlefish, and anchovies. They grow too big to be eaten by wading and diving birds like herons and kingfishers, but must watch out for sea lions, orcas, and seals. Many of them might be caught in fishing nets, but some will survive to begin the last dramatic part of their life cycle.

For reasons known only to the salmon, big schools of these fish will leave the ocean and gather at the mouth of a river. There are many rivers that flow into the ocean. The fish will know which river is the right one for them by the chemical smell of the water that they learned years before. It is a dangerous thing to do, to gather in such great numbers. Eagles, bears, sea gulls, sea lions, fishermen, all know that the fish are coming and wait for a chance to catch them.

But the salmon come anyway. They wait for the first heavy rain that makes the river rise and changes its smell and color. Then the salmon leave the sea forever, from salt water back to fresh. Once they start the swim upriver, they do not eat. Their bodies begin another change in shape and color. The chinook salmon turn purple and moss green. The sockeye become bright red. Snouts grow long and curved like a hook. Teeth grow sharp and pointed.

The salmon jump and push through the water with flicks of their tails. They leap over waterfalls and huge rocks. The fish are in a hurry, living off the last fat and energy in their bodies. Every day they swim twenty or thirty miles. Scars show where they have slammed into rocks or escaped the claws of a hungry bear. The skin thickens and fish scales disappear. The salmon are tired and wearing out, but they do not stop. They know where they are going and will do anything they can to get there.

There are many streams that flow into the big river. Each fish turns off into the stream of its birth, the one that it remembers by the special chemical smell. If the water starts to get shallow, the fish can wiggle across the rocky bottom for a short distance. If it is a hot, dry year without enough water, they will not be able to complete their journey. But this time they swim through a clean, cool flow of water. Finally they come to the area of the gravel beds where they were born.

The female salmon digs a nest by slapping her tail in the gravel. The nest might be very big, twice as long as her body. A large chinook can make a nest eighteen inches deep. A male swims up next to her and they are ready to spawn. She lays round, pink salmon eggs in the hole. The male fish fertilizes the eggs with milt, a white liquid from his body. Then the female digs another nest

Salmon Cycle

Adult returns to stream

Adult (may stay
in the ocean
one to five years)

Smolt: salmon ready
to go to the ocean

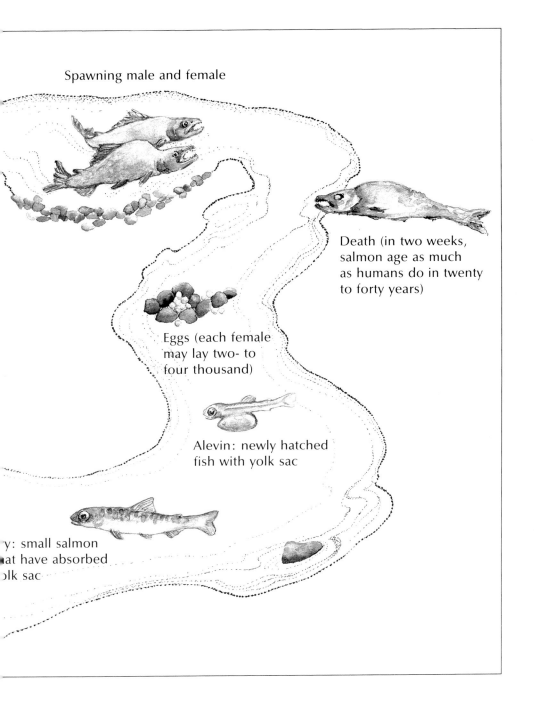

Spawning male and female

Death (in two weeks, salmon age as much as humans do in twenty to forty years)

Eggs (each female may lay two- to four thousand)

Alevin: newly hatched fish with yolk sac

y: small salmon
at have absorbed
olk sac

upstream. She may dig many nests over several days. Each time she digs a new nest, she covers up an old one with the gravel that she sweeps up from the bottom. This whole area of nest building is called a redd. Most of the salmon eggs remain safely hidden in the dark spaces between the gravel until they are ready to hatch.

The spawned-out fish are tired, battered, and starting to rot. They drift backward with the current and soon die in the stream. Some dead fish are eaten by bears and birds. Others rot in the water and leave minerals from the ocean for the trees to absorb. The dead fish also provide food for hungry plankton. This helps the new salmon fry that will need plenty of plankton to eat in a few months. Some of the dead fish might even become a nest for tiny white insect eggs that hatch on the body and then eat it for their very first meal.

And the journey of the salmon comes to an end, life to death, death to life again. This is how the salmon cycle works under the best of conditions. It is part of a good balance of all things in nature.

2

Salmon in History

For thousands and thousands of years, the cycle of the salmon worked very well. Salmon filled the rivers and were a most important food for the Plateau and Northwest Coast Indians. Different tribes lived along the water wherever they could find this fish. They knew all the habits of the fish just as they knew many things about nature. They could catch and preserve as many as a thousand fish per family each year.

The Indians understood the cycle of the salmon differently from the way scientists do. They thought the salmon were people who could change into a fish and back to people, over and over again. Some believed the salmon people lived in five different villages in the sea and that each tribe had its own time and place for returning to the streams to lay eggs.

Sockeye run, Alaska. *Copyright Gregory T. Ruggerone.*

The Indians had great respect for the salmon. Every year they watched for the return of the first fish on its run back from the sea. They felt this first fish was a scout for the rest of the village. When it arrived and was caught, the Indians held a special First Salmon Ceremony. In their own way, each tribe thanked the fish for coming back to feed them another year. There was singing and dancing, and the fish was asked to tell the others that it was treated well so other fish would follow. Some gave this fish gifts of eagle feathers and red ochre, a valuable clay used for painting. Others made sure to return all the bones to the water so that the salmon people would not be offended. They gave the fish honorary names like Lightning of the River and Great Jumper.

The rules for catching, cleaning, and cooking the salmon came from Indian myths. The wise, inventive creature Coyote is in several stories about the salmon. Coyote teaches many things about this fish, including how to share, be patient, and not be greedy.

One story tells about two women who have all the salmon penned up for themselves. Coyote does not like this. He changes himself into a baby so that the women will let him into their house. When they leave, he sets to work, digging with a stick to let the water and fish out of

Salmon Spirit. Copyright Roger Fernandes. This illustration by an Indian artist of the Lower Elwha Klallam nation symbolizes the importance of salmon to the Indians.

the pen and into the river so that everyone can share these fish. Then he transforms the women into two swallows who must fly above the river when the salmon return to spawn.

In another story, Coyote makes a waterfall so that the salmon will have to jump high and be easier to catch. He also makes a magic fish trap but is too impatient when he uses it. The trap is offended and stops working. Now the people must fish at the waterfalls using spears and dip nets.

One time, Coyote asks for the daughter of Beaver. Beaver agrees because he knows that Coyote is wise and smart and he will always have plenty of salmon to eat. Coyote makes changes in the river so that there will be many salmon to catch easily. Soon the salmon are so thick that Beaver cannot throw a stick into the water without hitting a fish. Coyote makes Beaver the Salmon Chief and tells him that he must never be greedy with the salmon and not let anyone else be greedy either. He must share the salmon with all the tribes who come.

The salmon became the most important part of the culture of the tribes on the rivers and coast in the Northwest. They caught many salmon and wasted none of it.

The heads and tails were eaten fresh. Much of the fish was dried or smoked and eaten later. Sometimes they cooked it in baskets of water, made to boil by adding hot rocks from the fire. Sometimes they split the fish and roasted it on cedar sticks next to a fire. They caught the oil that dripped from the cooking and licked it off their fingers. In winter, salmon dipped in oil was a favorite food.

They also dried and ate salmon eggs. Some made salmon egg soup. A tribe might have as many as two hundred ways to prepare salmon because it was so important to them.

Sometimes dried fish was pounded into powder and mixed with berries to make pemmican, a food that could be saved to eat in the winter. Great amounts of fish were taken from The Dalles on the Columbia River. The Dalles was a long stretch of the river with many waterfalls and rapids and very good for fishing. Many tribes gathered there to fish and trade. Eighty or ninety pounds of pemmican was a good trade for a horse from the Plains Indians.

The Indians used fish skins to make clothing and boots and also used the skin as a waterproof lining for storage baskets. They used fish bones to make needles and

Boots made from salmon skin by a Mainland Southwest Alaska Eskimo. *Courtesy Thomas Burke Memorial Washington State Museum, no. 7142A.*

combs. Paints were mixed with salmon egg oil. They even learned how to chew on the skin of the salmon, heat it in a clam shell until it was liquid, and then use it as a glue.

They made beautiful baskets for cooking and storing the fish. They made dip nets out of nettles and harpoons from bone and straight pieces of pine. They built fences in rivers called weirs, and carved clubs and long canoes, all things to help them in catching salmon. They might spend an entire month grinding a hole in a rock

Dip net fishing. *Courtesy University of Washington Libraries, Special Collections Division, no. NA 208.*

Indian Methods of Fishing

Salmon caught at a weir using a spear and a dip net.

Indian Methods of Cooking Salmon

Boiling in a basket using hot rocks to heat water

Roasting on a cooking stick

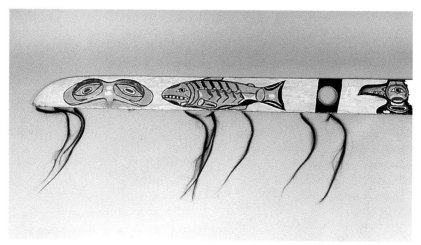

Ceremonial dance staff with salmon design, made by a Tlingit artist. *no. 2.5E519.*

Wooden sculpture of salmon, from the Nuu-chah-nulth people. *no. 2.5E1025.*

All photos on these two pages courtesy of the Thomas Burke Memorial Washington State Museum.

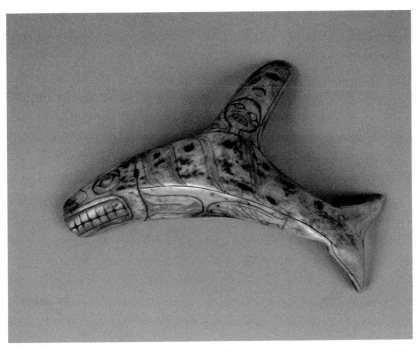

Amulet depicting killer whale and salmon, by a Haida artist. *no. 963.*

to make a net weight to hold a fishing net deep under water.

The salmon is a part of Indian designs, myths, ceremonies, and songs and reveals the Indians' deep respect for nature. These people understood that the salmon was important to other creatures as well. They carved eagles with salmon in their talons, orcas with salmon in their bellies. They caught only the amount of salmon that they

Some of the Creatures That Depend on Salmon for Food

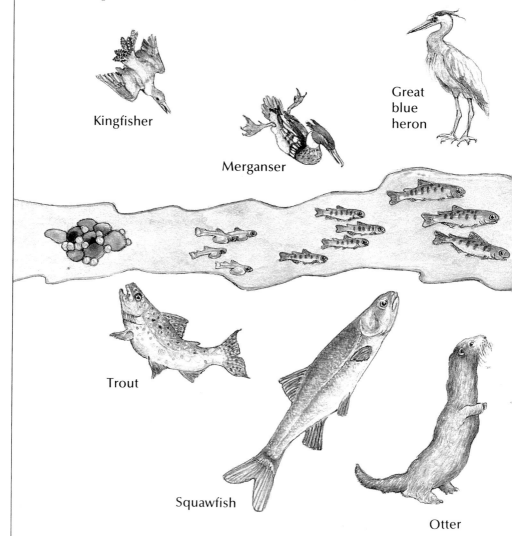

Kingfisher

Merganser

Great blue heron

Trout

Squawfish

Otter

Eagle

Sea gull

Human

Bear

Seal

Orca

needed. In return, the fish were thick and plentiful in the streams. Because these tribes did not have to worry about food supplies, they had time to develop great cultures with sculpture and rock paintings, totem poles, fine baskets, and longhouses of cedar or woven plants.

When Lewis and Clark traveled along the Columbia River in 1805, they wrote about "the great quantities of salmon" and "multitudes of this fish." They said that "they float in such quantity that the Indians have only to collect, split, and dry them on scaffolds." It was the first time these explorers had eaten salmon, and they liked it very much. There was enough fish to dry for fuel and dog food. In Alaska, dogs on sled teams were fed one fish each day. When Admiral Byrd went on his second Antarctic expedition, he took two thousand pounds of dried pemmican for his men and sled dogs. Early fur traders also knew about this huge number of fish. They were unwilling to put their boats into the Fraser River when the sockeye salmon returned to spawn. They were afraid the huge numbers of leaping fish might tip them over.

After Lewis and Clark explored the Northwest, many new people came to settle this area. These people did not know the cycle of the salmon. They did not understand the great wild rivers and all the creatures that lived nearby. They did not hear the Coyote stories that might teach them to share and not be greedy. As they came in great numbers over a hundred years ago, the story of the salmon began to change.

3

Salmon in Trouble

Remember the Indian myth where Coyote makes Beaver the Salmon Chief? When the fur trappers first came to the Northwest in the nineteenth century, they did not know that the beaver was an important animal. They did not know that chewing on trees and building dams was important for the wild rivers and streams and the cycle of the salmon.

Fur trappers were more interested in the European fashion of wearing hats. The best hats were made from beaver fur, and everybody wanted one. Trappers could make a lot of money selling beaver furs they had collected. They were very good at this job. By the middle of the nineteenth century there were hardly any beavers left in the streams.

When beavers build small dams, the deep water around them becomes a place where salmon can rest and

Sockeye in shallow water, Alaska. *Copyright Gregory T. Ruggerone.*

hide. When beavers knock wood chips and small trees and leaves into the water, these things become food for plankton, which salmon fry will eat. Beavers make ponds and marshes and do lots of important work around streams. When the beavers disappeared, all the work they did for the water system was gone too. This was not good for the salmon.

Then settlers came to build ranches and farms. To do this, they chopped down great numbers of trees. When it rained, the topsoil from the plowed land washed into the streams and covered the gravel beds. Salmon eggs and alevin were buried in this mud and died. Some of the ranchers had great herds of cattle. When these herds drank in the streams, they trampled many more salmon and ruined the gravel beds. In some places, without the shade of trees and other plants, the streams got too hot and more salmon died.

Trouble for the salmon continued with the Gold Rush in 1858. Huge areas of land were stripped, dug up, and then forgotten. Acres of loose topsoil washed down into the streams, covering more spawning beds and suffocating more baby salmon.

Things got worse after 1864. The Hume brothers and Andrew Hapgood opened up the first salmon cannery. Business was slow at first, but then it boomed. Soon

Cannery. *Courtesy Whatcom Museum of History and Art, Bellingham, Washington.*

there were canneries up and down the coast, dozens of them on the Columbia River and over six hundred thousand cases of salmon canned in a good year. Suddenly there were far too many people interested in catching the salmon. They became so valuable that river pirates began to highjack boatloads of fish.

The cannery people did not understand the whole salmon cycle. The only thing they noticed was the great numbers of fish that gathered at the mouths of rivers to swim upstream. They designed huge traps and fish wheels to catch them all. They hired many people to handle the fish and then wasted most of the salmon by using only the bellies. The leftover parts were dumped back into the water, and soon the water became very polluted.

In some years, there were far too many fish for the canneries to handle. They closed early in the day and turned fishermen away. The extra fish, many of them females filled with eggs, were pushed overboard to rot. One day in 1897 a huge run of salmon came up the river. Millions of fish were overcaught. These were dumped back into the water. The winds and tides washed the dead fish up on the riverbank. Soon stinking, rotten bodies were two feet deep and more than two hundred feet wide. It was a huge pollution and health problem and a big waste of fish. It caused great damage to the salmon in this river.

One good thing did happen because of the overfishing by the canneries. People began to band together and fight

Twenty-five-thousand fish on cannery floor, Washington. *Courtesy Whatcom Museum of History and Art, Bellingham, Washington.*

against the fish traps. They developed a public feeling that the fish belonged to all people and not just a few wealthy cannery owners.

Many Indian tribes continued to fish for salmon in the ways they had done for thousands of years. They tried to tell the new people how important the fish were to them and for all people. One Indian said that if he could not eat salmon for three days in a row, he would die. In treaties made in 1884 and 1885, the tribes were told they could always share in the catch of salmon.

In 1871, Congress appointed a commission to find out why so many salmon were disappearing from the rivers. They discovered that too many fish were being caught, the water was polluted, and the streambeds were being destroyed. They did not fix these problems. Instead they thought it might be a good idea to raise salmon in fish hatcheries. A hatchery is a group of buildings and ponds where salmon and other fish can be hatched, fed, and then put into a stream. The first hatchery on the Columbia River was built in 1877, and many have been built since then. But none of them have really given the salmon as much help as they need because hatcheries do not fix the problems in the water system where the salmon must live. Also, hatchery fish are not as strong or clever as wild salmon.

Eventually most of the canneries closed down and the huge fish traps were not allowed, but problems for the salmon continued. Salmon need a swift, open river to travel through their cycle. But many people wanted to use the rivers for other things. Farmers put pipes into the water and pumped out huge volumes to irrigate their crops. Sometimes fish fry were swept up into the irrigation system and left to die on the fields.

Other people wanted to build dams. Dams are huge concrete structures that block a river and use the flow of water to make electricity. They are a good way to make electric power, but they also change rivers. Dams create a huge backup of water that floods over rapids and waterfalls and turns the wild river into a series of warm, slow reservoir lakes. These smoothed-out rivers are good for waterskiing and boat transportation, even for flood control. But they are not good at all for the salmon.

Grand Coulee Dam was opened in 1941, a huge concrete wall in the Columbia River as high as a thirty-five-story building. When salmon that wanted to spawn reached this wall, they tried to jump over it. Salmon never turn back; they never quit. With worn-out bodies and the last of their energy, they slammed against this concrete wall until finally they died. There are over six hundred miles of spawning beds on the other side of this dam that have been lost to the salmon forever. Other dams have blocked off more gravel beds. Over one third of all spawning areas can no longer be reached, and many salmon runs have become extinct.

Some of the dams on salmon rivers have fish ladders,

a series of water steps that allow fish to swim up and around the concrete wall. Fish ladders are very long and to climb them takes many extra days of swimming. The old salmon cycle that worked for thousands of years never had to allow for this extra time. The slowdown is a disaster for salmon that must travel through several dams. Many fish run out of time and die before they can spawn.

The dams also cause problems for salmon fry when they swim downstream to the ocean. Some are chewed up in the great turbines of the dams. Others go over the spillways at the top and are stunned in the long fall to the lower level of the river. Sea gulls and other birds like to spend long, lazy days catching these injured fish. Sometimes the bubbly water at the bottom of these spillways gets too much nitrogen in it. When the fish breathe this bubbly water in through their gills, they can get "gas bubble disease." The fish get sick with bubbles in their blood vessels, and many die.

Some fry spend too much time in the reservoirs looking for a swift current to carry them downstream. If they stay too long, they will lose the urge to continue. Or they may get too warm and suffer from disease. These lakes are just too warm and slow for them. On the other hand, the huge squawfish prefers the reservoirs. There are many more squawfish now than could survive in the wild rivers. And squawfish love to eat little salmon.

What else could possibly make a problem for these fish? Sadly, there are other things. In 1913, a railroad line was built in Canada. A careless blast of dynamite started a big rock slide that blocked the river below. About ten million fish died when they could not swim up this river.

Salmon, like many other animals, are hurt when roads and cities and shopping malls are built and more trees cut down. Building projects put more silt into the streams, killing more salmon eggs or alevin. So many trees have been chopped down that for the salmon it must feel like the loss of millions of beaver. Gone are the twigs, needles, and leaves that float into the streams. Gone too are old fallen logs and clumps of roots that slow the water and make a quiet, safe resting place for the salmon. Gone with the slow-water spots are the areas where gravel can drop out of the current and make new beds for salmon eggs.

When the trees are gone, so is the shade. A stream can get very hot in direct sun. Salmon like the water to be fifty or sixty degrees Fahrenheit. If the water temperature climbs into the seventies, the fish will die.

Not only do the salmon like cool water but they like it

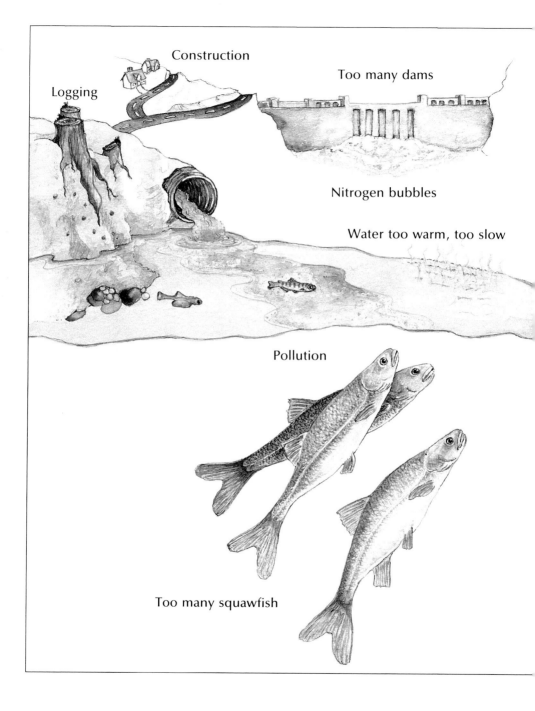

Logging

Construction

Too many dams

Nitrogen bubbles

Water too warm, too slow

Pollution

Too many squawfish

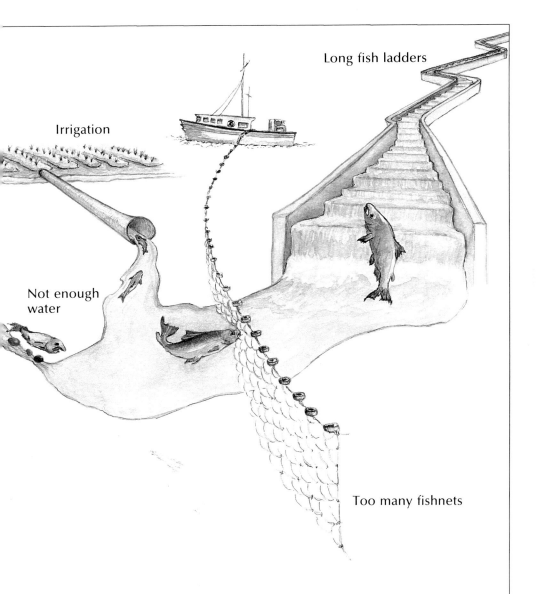

Irrigation

Long fish ladders

Not enough water

Too many fishnets

Salmon Cycle in Trouble

to be clean and clear. If the water gets too dirty, the salmon can't see their food. Heavy silt can also damage the gills of the fish. Many things get into water that are not good for salmon. Sewage, factory waste, fertilizers, car leaks, detergents, plastics, insect killers, all of these make life hard for the fish.

Fishing must also be added to the problem list. Fishermen from many different countries set up huge nets in the ocean to catch salmon. Other people might fish from small boats, or with fishing poles or nets. People everywhere like to eat this fish, and it is good protein, rich in vitamins and minerals. Some people like to catch salmon because it is fun and a challenge. Salmon are fighters— they never give up, and it can be a thrill to finally catch one. Indian tribes continue to catch fish in the ways that have always been so important to them. The problem is that there just aren't enough fish. Every fish that is caught is one less that can swim to its home stream to spawn.

The result of so many years of trouble is that many kinds of salmon are already extinct and others are in great danger. The Snake River sockeye salmon has been put on the endangered species list. In 1991 only four fish were able to make the nine-hundred-mile journey, past eight dams, to their spawning beds. Three of these were males, and one was a female called Eve. The Columbia

River system used to have at least sixteen million salmon. Now there are only about two million. Just three hundred thousand of these are wild salmon; the rest come from hatcheries. Salmon from other rivers are also in great trouble. Millions of wild salmon have disappeared.

Everything that happens along a water system affects the salmon. It also affects bears, eagles, sea lions, insects, fishing birds, people, trees, all life in or around the river. The story of the salmon tells us about precious things that have been lost and nature out of balance.

It is not a happy story. This is why so many people are trying to come up with good ideas that will help.

4

Salmon Rescue

The salmon problem is so big it seems to touch everyone. Because the salmon is endangered, some people are required by law to protect it. Others are involved because they care about the salmon and where it lives. Fish and wildlife agencies, loggers, members of Congress, fishermen, artists, Indian tribes, dam operators, governors, photographers, barge operators, farmers, scientists, environmentalists, writers, lawyers, concerned citizens—all are hard at work on a rescue plan for the salmon.

People looking for ways to help the salmon must ask some difficult questions. For instance, there is no doubt that most dams are here to stay. On the Columbia River they provide enough electricity for twelve cities the size of Seattle. So what can be done for all the young salmon that cannot survive a trip through the dams?

Someone came up with an idea about barges and tug-

Salmon barge near dam in Columbia River, Oregon. *Copyright Natalie Fobes.*

boats. Tugboats are always pushing barges loaded with wheat and other cargo on the rivers. Why not load them up with tiny salmon that could use a better way to get downstream?

This was an idea that was put into action. Salmon fry have been a cargo on the Columbia and Snake rivers since 1977. They are collected above the higher dams, put into tanks on barges, and then shipped past many of the dangers of the river. It has not been an easy thing to do because travel conditions must be just right. If the water does not flow properly around them, the fish will not be able to breathe. If the fish are too crowded or too hot, some will die. If they are all let out at the same place, smart birds and fish will soon be waiting to eat them up.

People have spent several years trying to make this new twist in the salmon cycle work as well as possible. There are now better ways to collect the fish and take them quickly out of the reservoir. If the river water becomes polluted, the barges can protect the fish from the problem. If the water has too much nitrogen, the barge system can filter it out and save many fish from gas bubble disease.

On the Snake and Columbia rivers, fifteen million young salmon were barged in 1992. At the peak of a run, when there might be millions of tiny fish in a day, six barges work to carry the fish downstream. It is an expensive ride. It costs about fifteen thousand dollars per round trip for each barge. All this money is paid by the people who use and enjoy electricity from the dams. At the beginnings and ends of the fish runs, when there might be only ten thousand or twenty thousand fish coming through, they can be picked up by trucks and driven past the dams. These trucks have water tanks lined and insulated like a huge thermos bottle. The truck rides cost much less, maybe around three hundred dollars.

Another idea has been to put screens in the dams to

keep the fish out of the turbines and help direct them to areas where they can be picked up for barging. This has not been an easy job either. The screens must be huge and strong so that they will not be crushed under the pressure of the river or broken by logs and other debris. They also must be cleaned often so that they do not get clogged. The first screens used seemed big enough—they were twenty feet high and about as heavy as twenty cars. But some of the fish managed to swim below these screens. Newer screens are forty feet high. At one dam alone, sixty-six of these huge screens will be needed.

Yet another idea has been to put ledges under the spillways at the dams. The water splashes off the ledges and slows down before reaching the bottom. The water is not so bubbly, and fewer fish suffer from gas bubble disease.

Since there are more pieces to the salmon problem, people keep asking more hard questions. What about the squawfish, the big fish that loves the warm, slow waters of the reservoirs? At just one dam, it was estimated that the squawfish ate about two million fry. This is far too many. The relationship between the squawfish and the salmon is out of balance.

A program was started to pay fishermen three dollars for each squawfish caught over eleven inches long. In the first year, twenty thousand of these fish were brought to

Squawfish

collection points. People could keep the fish or turn it in to be used for leather, fertilizer, or fish meal to feed the young salmon.

The people thinking about these ideas realize that none of the changes made at the dams will do much good if the salmon have big problems somewhere else. Several groups are being asked to take a close look at their part in the life-and-death drama of this fish.

One of these groups is the farmers. To make sure that the salmon have enough water, farmers may not take as much irrigation water from the rivers, especially in dry seasons. Some farmers are now taking a new look at what crops they should grow. Will there be enough water for thirsty potatoes? Maybe it's a good year to grow grains that don't need as much water. But there's more money to be earned from potatoes. Will we get much rain? Farmers have new decisions to make. They also have new expenses, like installing screens across irrigation pipes, keeping the fry in the streams, and not drawing them up on the land.

The people who raise cattle are thinking about ways to get water to their herds without letting them walk through the streambeds. A new concrete water channel has been designed for this job. The stream flows through the channel, and the cattle come there to drink. Good fencing keeps the animals out of the rest of the stream. Sometimes neighbors will get involved in helping someone make these changes for the salmon. They might bring a huge bag of nails, drive up with a bulldozer, or spend a day digging holes for the fence posts.

Loggers are also making changes. They are looking more carefully at hillsides to decide which trees to cut. They can be fined for such things as dragging logs across

Stream Rescue for the Salmon

Leave trees on steep hillsides to prevent erosion

Clean up garbage

Add gravel to weak banks to keep dirt from washing into stream

Replant logged areas with grass, bushes, and trees

Use fences and concrete water troughs to keep cattle out of stream

Leave logs and rocks in stream to make deep pools where fish can rest a gravel bed. They must leave a strip of uncut trees twenty-five feet wide on each side of the stream. Some think this area should be much greater, maybe one hundred feet. Loggers are being urged to leave enough trees to protect the land from washing away. There are many different opinions on just how many trees should be cut and where. These are not easy decisions. Trees left standing help to save the salmon and other animals that live in the forest. This also means fewer jobs for the loggers and less lumber to build furniture and houses.

Because of the troubled salmon, commercial and sport fishermen are dealing with a great drop in fishing business. Their part in the rescue plan includes many limits on the amounts and kinds of fish they may catch and where they may catch them. Sometimes they may not be allowed to catch any at all if threatened salmon are in the area. When there aren't enough salmon to go around, everyone starts to notice how many other people have. Canadians watch to see how many fish from their streams are caught in Alaska and Washington State. Fishermen in Puget Sound want to know how many Columbia River salmon are caught in Canadian waters. Other countries fish for the salmon in the open ocean, and it is not easy to get everyone to agree on which methods to use, or which fish to catch and how many.

Indian tribes are allowed to fish in areas where they have fished for thousands of years. Some non-Indians are unhappy about this, thinking that the tribes are getting too many fish. The tribes, however, have concerns of their own. They may fish only in the areas where they have fished in the past. If the fish runs become extinct in their area, they may not move somewhere else to catch other fish. They are deeply concerned about losing the salmon, which has been the center of their lives for thousands of years, and are actively involved in a huge effort to make sure that the salmon will be around for thousands of years to come.

One of the hardest questions involves the fish hatcheries. Millions of salmon have been released into streams from the hatchery programs. Unfortunately, some of these fish are weaker and carry diseases that they pass on to the wild fish. They compete with the wild fish for food. While wild fish learn to hide in tree roots and pools and dart out for a meal, hatchery fish often live in concrete ponds and always have plenty to eat. If they are overcrowded, they begin to fight with one another. Hatchery fish and wild fish are not learning the same things to survive. The fish are not equal. Gradually people are changing their ideas about hatcheries and looking for the best ways to make them part of the rescue plan.

Feeding chum fry in incubator with a spring device that delivers constant food for twelve hours. *Copyright Brenda Z. Guiberson.*

Some people are trying a new way to raise fish with a small hatchery built right into the stream. The little hatchery has three small boxes—one to filter the water, one to raise the eggs and alevin, and one used as a safe place to feed the fry until they are released into the stream. Everyone hopes, of course, that the fish will come back to build a new run of fish.

The forestry and fishery agencies have also changed their ideas about logs in the streams. Ten years ago, they were taking logs out of the water because they thought of them as barriers to the salmon. With better informa-

Streamside incubator for chum to reestablish run in Salmon Creek, Washington. Volunteers built the incubator and attend to it almost daily. *Copyright Brenda Z. Guiberson.*

tion, they now have a program to put the logs back. What better information did they get? A study showed that salmon fry do best in streams with the largest number of beavers. The beaver is important again! Beaver, the Salmon Chief, is no longer forgotten.

The best part of the salmon rescue plan is that people are willing to try something new if an old idea doesn't work. And they will go back to the old if the new idea is wrong. How do they know when to make these changes? This is where the scientists and careful observers of nature come in. They study the water systems and count and measure the fish. They are always checking and re-checking every part of the salmon cycle. This constant information helps to keep the salmon rescue plan headed in the right direction.

Salmon Science

This salmon story is about five kinds of Pacific salmon: chinook, sockeye, coho, chum, and pink. All of these salmon are alike in many ways. They have the same shape, the same number of fins, and the same cycle of life.

These salmon are also different from one another. The chinook are the biggest—the record is 126 pounds. The pinks are very small, maybe only two or three pounds. Coho are great jumpers, but the chum are not. Some sockeye will spend a year or two in a lake, while chum and pink fry move right out to sea.

Even the same kind of salmon can be different from one another. Coho from hatcheries are different from those that are wild. Chinook that spawn in the spring have more oil and more color than chinook that spawn in the fall. Sockeye that look the same might be different from one another because one spends more years in the ocean or comes from colder water, steeper streams, longer rivers, or streams with beaver ponds.

These small differences are hard to discover but are very important. The fish scientists will do almost anything to find out the details about each group of fish. If it seems helpful to count young salmon in the middle of a snowy winter, a scientist will show up with a wet suit, a snorkel, and a camera for the job. Another scientist might go up in a helicopter to see if any fish are at the mouth of a river. Some scientists will travel on huge ships to look for salmon in the middle of the ocean. Others will camp along streams with cameras, thermometers, notebooks, and plenty of glass jars to collect water samples. They will measure and record everything that they see. How big is the gravel in this creek? What happens to the coho fry in a storm? Where do these chum go in the ocean? Why are the fish smaller this year? How do we find out? Can we fix it?

Scientists are always asking questions like these. They look at details and then try to figure out what it all means. For instance, one scientist watched hundreds of bears, eagles, and sea gulls come to a stream in Alaska to eat salmon. This was easy to understand. These animals know the fish are coming and depend on them for food.

Scientist looking for chinook smolt in a creek, Idaho. *Copyright Natalie Fobes.*

Bears will eat many salmon before they hibernate for the winter.

One day the scientist noticed small white specks around the eyes and mouth of a dead fish. This was a bit of mystery. He took a picture and returned the next day. The only thing left of the fish was the skeleton. *Click*, he took another picture and decided to study more dead fish along the stream. He discovered that the white specks were the eggs of a fly. When the insects hatched, their first meal was the salmon, and they could eat the fish down to the bone in a very short time. The scientist then had to ask, What does this all mean? His answer was that at least in this stream, in this particular place in Alaska, the fly has a part in the cycle of the salmon.

When these scientists study a stream, they look for all the things that would be important to the salmon in it. Suppose one scientist studies stream A. She notices that the stream is very steep and is a long swim from the ocean. There are many natural waterfalls to jump. The gravel in the bed is very big because the fast water washes away the small pieces. What does all this mean to the scientist? She understands that the fish who come to this stream must be able to swim a long distance, jump high many times, and have a strong tail to sweep away the heavy gravel. If she counts only ten fish that come to

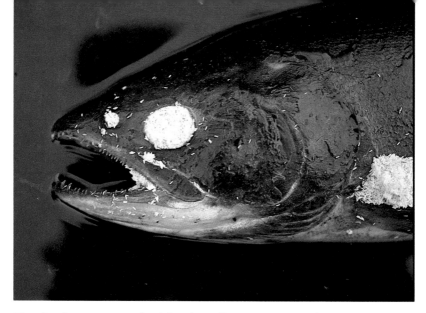

Dead salmon covered with white fly eggs. *Copyright Gregory T. Ruggerone.*

spawn in this stream, she is deeply concerned about the survival of these fish.

She goes downriver to look at stream B. This stream is not so steep, but the temperature is quite cold. Water samples show that there is very little plankton to eat. Salmon here must be able to survive in cold water. Because there is so little food, the fry should be the kind that swim right out to the ocean. The scientist counts only fifteen fish that return to spawn and is very concerned about these fish too.

Farther downriver she studies stream C. The water here is a bit warmer; the swim from the ocean is short;

The same salmon a short time later, eaten by newly hatched flies. *Copyright Gregory T. Ruggerone.*

there are no waterfalls but plenty of plankton. There are also two big beaver ponds where fry can find food and protection over the winter. She counts at least one thousand fish that return to spawn in this stream and is happy to see a group of fish that is doing so well.

She talks to other scientists. What is happening to the fish in streams A and B? They look for answers and find that usually the fish from all three streams are counted together at the mouth of the river. About two thousand fish return to spawn, and fishermen are allowed to catch half of them. Until now, no one really knew how many salmon went to each different stream. Now they can see

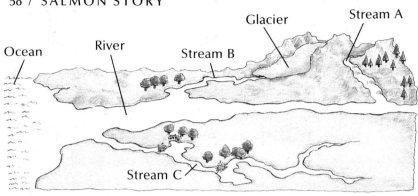

Scientists can learn many things by observing the habits of salmon from different streams

that the runs in streams A and B are very different. What can possibly be done to protect these fish?

The scientists would look for more information. They might find a week in the year when fish only from stream C are in the river. What if they limited fishing to that week only? Or they could weigh and measure fish from each stream. If fish from stream C are the biggest, they might be able to find a size of fishing net that could catch only the larger fish and let the smaller ones swim by. Another plan might be to allow fishing only in stream C and nowhere else. What else could they do? The scientists must choose something quickly and then keep checking and counting to make sure that this part of the rescue plan works as well as it should.

Some details about the salmon can be learned by studying the streams, but others are harder to discover. For instance, how old is the fish? How many years did it spend in the ocean? Did it get enough to eat? Scientists can't ask a salmon about these things, but they want to know. How can they find out?

This fishnet catches only the larger fish, letting the smaller ones swim by.

Answers to these particular questions can be found on the scales of a salmon. Scientists use tweezers to remove a scale from a fish, melt an image of this scale onto a piece of acetate and project the image onto a screen. The scale can also be studied under a microscope. With a careful look at just a single scale, scientists can often tell the kind and age of the fish, how big it has been at other stages of its life, and where it has been living.

The very smallest circle on a fish scale shows up when the fish is a fry, just beginning to get scales. As the salmon grows, more rings are added. Soon there is a ring that is all broken up into little lines. This is the point when the fry becomes a smolt and leaves fresh water to go into the ocean. This change, which involves a new way for the skin and kidneys to work, is very hard on the fish, and the scientists can see how hard it is right there on the scales.

After swimming into the ocean, the salmon starts to grow at a much faster rate with all the new food available. A smolt might double in size in just a few weeks. The rings, ridges of new growth, get thicker and farther apart because the salmon is growing so much. During the winter, less food is available and the growth rate slows down. Now the lines on the scales are much closer together. Each time the lines get close together means another winter has passed in the ocean.

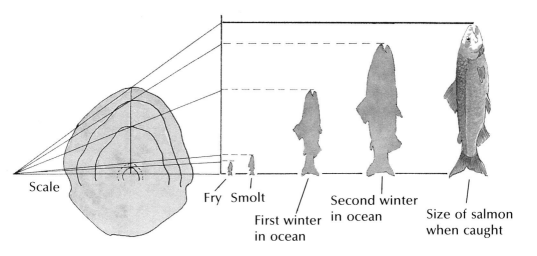

Scale

Fry Smolt

First winter
in ocean

Second winter
in ocean

Size of salmon
when caught

Scientists can estimate the size of a salmon at different stages in its life by the ridges on a single scale from its body.

What helps the scientists the most is to figure out the salmon age of the fish. Salmon age is not like people age. It is a number that tells where the salmon has lived and might even be used to tell what lake or stream it is from. A salmon that has spent one year in fresh water and two years in the ocean is given the age of 1.2. A salmon that goes right out to the ocean as a fry and then spends three years in the sea is given the age of 0.3. Coho, chum, chinook, and sockeye can have several different ages, depending on when and where they spawn. Pinks, however, are always given the age of 0.1. Pinks spend almost no time in fresh water and always return after one winter in the ocean. Scientists would be amazed to find a pink with any age different than 0.1. If they did, they would look everywhere to find out the reason for this change.

Each year, scientists look at the salmon ages of many fish and then see if the fish are growing as they should. An interesting thing happened in 1983, when a warm, southern current in the ocean, called El Niño, moved up into the cold water of the northern Pacific Ocean. When this current shifted, it was very hard on all the creatures that live in colder water. The salmon had trouble finding the right things to eat. In that year, the scientists who read salmon scales saw ocean growth rings that were broken into small lines because of the extra stress on the hungry fish. Many salmon died. The ones who survived were not as big as they had been in other years, when there was more to eat.

Another good way to get information about a salmon is to put a tag on the fish. This method works only if the person who catches the fish returns the tag to the scientists and tells them where and when the fish was caught.

Sometimes fish are tagged at hatcheries. This tag is a teeny wire that is shorter than a dash (–) and thin as a strand of hair. The wire has a code on it that tells special things about the fish, like what hatchery it is from and

Salmon Anatomy

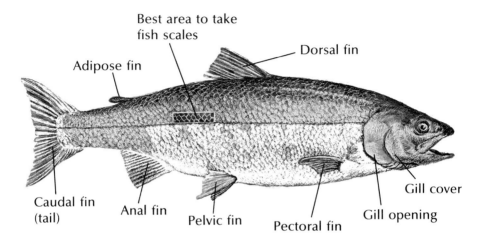

any special diet it may have been fed. These coded-wire tags are pushed into the heads of young fish and are not easy to see. To help the fishermen know which fish carry a tag, the hatchery workers also clip off the small, round adipose fin of each fish.

Scientists are eager to get back as many of these tags as possible. Sometimes they will wait at the fishing docks to collect the heads of tagged fish as soon as the fishermen come in. If the scientists can't be at the docks, they want the fishermen to throw the fish heads into a plastic bag with lots of salt to preserve them and mail the package right to the fisheries department.

Sometimes larger fish are caught and tagged by scientists way out in the ocean. Japanese, Russian, and North American scientists are all involved in catching salmon and attaching a tag near the dorsal, or back, fin of the fish. These tags are about the size of a dime and are easy to see. After tagging, the fish are released to swim wherever they might want to go in the ocean. Again, fishermen are asked to return these tags when the fish are caught. Contests with big prize money are held to get the attention of as many fishermen as possible.

Occasionally a tag shows up that is a total mystery. One tag was recovered in a tin of canned salmon. Another tag was found under a skunk cabbage in Maine! But most recovered tags provide valuable information for the scientists. For instance, one tag told scientists that a certain chinook from the Columbia River ended up very far north in the central Bering Sea, maybe something that had never happened before. Why? How? This fact, or maybe another, could lead to something new and better in the salmon rescue plan.

Another type of tag used by the scientists is the PIT (Passive Integrated Transponder) tag. This tag takes the salmon into the computer age. Whenever a salmon with a PIT tag swims around dams and other areas with the right equipment, the tagged fish will transmit information, like who they are, where they come from, and what they ate, just the kind of things the scientists always want to know. These tags are much more expensive than coded-wire tags but are also much better, since the tags can be read without killing the fish.

Every year scientists read thousands of salmon scales, put tags on millions of fish, and study many streams to see what is new in the cycle of the salmon. The salmon knows best what it needs to survive, and the scientists seem to be asking the fish for answers. They are not asking just one fish, but all salmon, from each stream, from each area, that has its own story to tell. Everyone in the salmon rescue plan is finding that it is much better to discover what each salmon needs to survive than to try to replace a fish once it is gone.

The story of the salmon will always continue. It tells about how well we take care of the places we live, what happens when we change things, how much clean water is left when we are done. All living things—plants, animals, humans—need the same healthy water system. If the strong, determined salmon is in great trouble, how many other creatures are in trouble? The salmon have a very important story to tell.

Selected Bibliography

Andrews, Chris, Adrian Exell, and Neville Carrington. *The Manual of Fish Health.* New Jersey: Tetra Press, 1988.

Ashwell, Reg. *Coast Salish: Their Art, Culture and Legends.* Seattle: Hancock House Publications, Inc., 1978.

Boas, Franz. *Kwakiutl Ethnography.* Chicago: University of Chicago Press, 1966.

Browning, Robert J. *Fisheries of the North Pacific.* Alaska Northwest Publishing Company, 1974, 1980.

Caras, Roger. *Sockeye: The Life of the Pacific Salmon.* New York: Dial Press, 1975.

Childerhose, R.J., and Marj Trim. *Pacific Salmon.* Vancouver, BC: Douglas & McIntyre Ltd., 1981.

Clark, Ella E. *Indian Legends of the Pacific Northwest.* Berkeley: University of California Press, 1953.

Cone, Molly. *Come Back, Salmon.* San Francisco: Sierra Club Books for Children, 1992.

Crandall, Julie V. *The Story of Pacific Salmon.* Portland, OR: Binford & Mort, 1946.

Groot, C., and L. Margolis, eds. *Pacific Salmon Life Histories.* Vancouver, BC: University of British Columbia Press, 1991.

Gunther, Erna. *Art in the Life of the Northwest Coast Indians: With a Catalog of the Rasmussen Collection of Northwest Indian Art at the Portland*

Art Museum. Seattle: Superior Publishing Company, 1966.

Holm, Bill. *Spirit and Ancestor.* Seattle: Burke Museum and University of Washington Press, 1987.

Kirk, Ruth. *Wisdom of the Elders: Native Traditions on the Northwest Coast.* Vancouver and Toronto: Douglas & McIntyre, 1986.

McConkey, Lois. *Sea and Cedar: How the Northwest Coast Indians Lived.* Seattle: Madrona Press, 1973.

McDowell, Jeanne. "A Race to Rescue the Salmon." *Time* (March 2, 1992): 59–60.

McKervill, Hugh W. *The Salmon People.* Canada: Gray's Publishing Ltd., 1967.

McNamee, Thomas. *Nature First.* Boulder, CO: Roberts Rinehart, Inc. Publishers, 1987.

Mosher, Kenneth H. "Identification of Pacific Salmon and Steelhead Trout by Scale Characteristics." Seattle: Bureau of Commercial Fisheries, 1969.

Nehlsen, Willa, Jack E. Williams, and James A. Lichatowich. "Pacific Salmon at the Crossroads." *Trout* (Winter 1992): 21–55.

Netboy, Anthony. *The Salmon: Their Fight for Survival.* Boston: Houghton Mifflin Company, 1974.

Porter, Frank W. III., *The Coast Salish Peoples.* New York: Chelsea House Publishers, 1989.

Ramsey, Jarold, ed. *Coyote Was Going There: Indian Literature of the Oregon Country.* Seattle: University of Washington Press, 1977.

Ronda, James P. *Lewis and Clark Among the Indians.* Lincoln: University of Nebraska Press, 1984.

Royce, William F. *Introduction to the Fishery Sciences.* New York: Academic Press, Inc., 1972.

Shapiro, Sidney, ed. *Our Changing Fisheries.* Washington, DC: Government Printing Office, 1971.

Smith, Courtland L. *Salmon Fishers of the Columbia.* Corvallis: Oregon State University Press, 1979.

Steelquist, Robert. *Field Guide to the Pacific Salmon.* Seattle: Sasquatch Books, 1992.

Stouder, Scott. "Coho Salmon Rehabilitation." *Salmon Trout Steelheader* (August–September 1992): 30–31.

Swan, James G. *The Haidah Indians of Queen Charlotte's Islands (1874).*

Seattle: The Shorey Book Store, 1964.

Teit, James A., and Franz Boas. *The Okanagon: An Extract from the Salishan Tribes of the Western Plateaus (1927–28)*. Seattle: The Shorey Book Store, 1973.

Urquhart, Jennifer. *Animals That Travel*. Washington, DC: National Geographic Society, 1982.

Van Dyk, Jere. "Long Journey of the Pacific Salmon." *National Geographic* (July 1990): 3–37.

Wallace, David Rains. *Life in the Balance*. San Diego: Harcourt Brace Jovanovich, 1987.

Wright, Robin K., ed. *A Time of Gathering*. Seattle: Burke Museum and University of Washington Press, 1991.

Index

Boldface indicates picture.

Here's a list of other nonfiction
Redfeather Books from Henry Holt

Alligators: A Success Story
by Patricia Lauber

Exploring an Ocean Tide Pool
by Jeanne Bendick

*Great Whales: The Gentle Giants
by Patricia Lauber

*Snakes: Their Place in the Sun
by Robert M. McClung

*Available in paperback

EDUCATION